FROM THE
BAROQUE
DUETS FOR CLARINET

Thirty-eight duets from the works of
Wilhelm Friedemann Bach • Jean-Marie Leclair • Georg Phillip Telemann

Compiled and Edited by
H. VOXMAN

T0052398

CONTENTS

ISBN 978-0-634-09417-0

RUBANK®

HAL•LEONARD®
CORPORATION
7777 W. BLUEMOUND RD. P.O. BOX 13819 MILWAUKEE, WI 53213

Visit Hal Leonard Online at
www.halleonard.com

PREFACE

The earliest known clarinet duets are in a collection published ca. 1715-1716 by Chez Estienne Roger & Le Cene Libraire in Amsterdam. The title page reads:

AIRS A DEUX CHALUMEAUX
Deux Trompettes, deux Haubois, deux Violons,
deux Flûtes, deux Clarinelles, ou Cors de Chasse
DEDIEZ `A
MONSIEUR HENRY IPERMAN.
LIVRE PREMIER

It is very unlikely that clarinets were ever called "clarinelles." When I used high magnification on the *ll*, I found them to be *tt*.

Subsequent decades saw a number of duet publications—in early method books, and separately. Some of the more significant composers were C.P.E. Bach, Michel Yost, Jean-Xavier Lefèvre, Anton Stadler, Jan Stefani, and Amand Vanderhagen.

An excellent account of the early history of the clarinet duet is David Randall's "A Comprehensive Performance Project in Clarinet Literature, with an Essay on the Clarinet Duet from 1715 to 1825," published by the University of Iowa, Iowa City, IA.

Much of the published duet music of this period has few dynamic markings. I have added a number of these, as well as articulations.

WILHELM FRIEDEMANN BACH (1710-1784) was the second son of Johann Sebastian and Maria Barbara Bach. He entered Leipzig University in 1723. In 1733 he was appointed organist at St. Sophia's Church in Dresden. He was also employed in Halle, then in 1770 left for Brunswick, where he had difficulty finding employment. He moved to Berlin in 1774, taught and gave organ lessons, but, as one writer phrased it, "fell into poverty."

He composed a sizeable body of church music, secular cantatas, and songs. His instrumental music included symphonies, violin and flute concertos, and much keyboard music.

The fifteen duets in this collection come from movements in his *Six Duets for Two Flutes*. Performers will gain a useful knowledge of the long appoggiatura, one of the most widely employed embellishments in the period. It was still used by Beethoven as late as his duets for clarinet and bassoon.

JEAN-MARIE LECLAIR "l'aine" ("the elder") was born in Lyon, France, in 1697. In 1722, he went to Turin to work as a ballet master, where he also did some composing. He began intensive study of the violin while playing in the Paris Opera orchestra from 1729-1731. Later he established himself in Paris as an excellent soloist and member of the royal orchestra, and composed and published a number of his works—mostly sonatas and concertos for violin. He was regarded as the greatest French writer for violin of his time and one of its finest performers.

Leclair wrote no works for the clarinet. The ten duets in this collection come from his Opus 3 and Opus 12 for two violins. His works for violin have a rather jolly character. Unfortunately, his life ended otherwise. He was stabbed to death in his home. There was no robbery. The French Archives Nationales believed his nephew may have been the assailant.

GEORG PHILIPP TELEMANN (1681-1767) After early study of languages and science at Leipzig University, he was appointed organist at the new church there, and founded a *collegium musicum*. He served in a number of positions in various German cities, but returned to Hamburg in 1721, where he held a number of prestigious posts. He died there in 1767, more famous (at the time) than J.S. Bach.

It has been estimated that Telemann wrote over 3,000 compositions. The most popular of his compositions are what he called *Tafelmusik* ("table music"), a great variety of solo and chamber music for various combinations. Although he used the clarinet in some of his chamber music, he wrote no clarinet duets. The thirteen in this collection are based on his flute duets.

H. VOXMAN

Fifteen Duets

Wilhelm Friedemann Bach
(1710–1784)

6

2

Vivace

Allegro mà non troppo

12

4

Gigue

22

Adagio ma non molto

24

26

Lamentabile

10

Presto   (Play ♪♪ figure as ♪³♪)

11

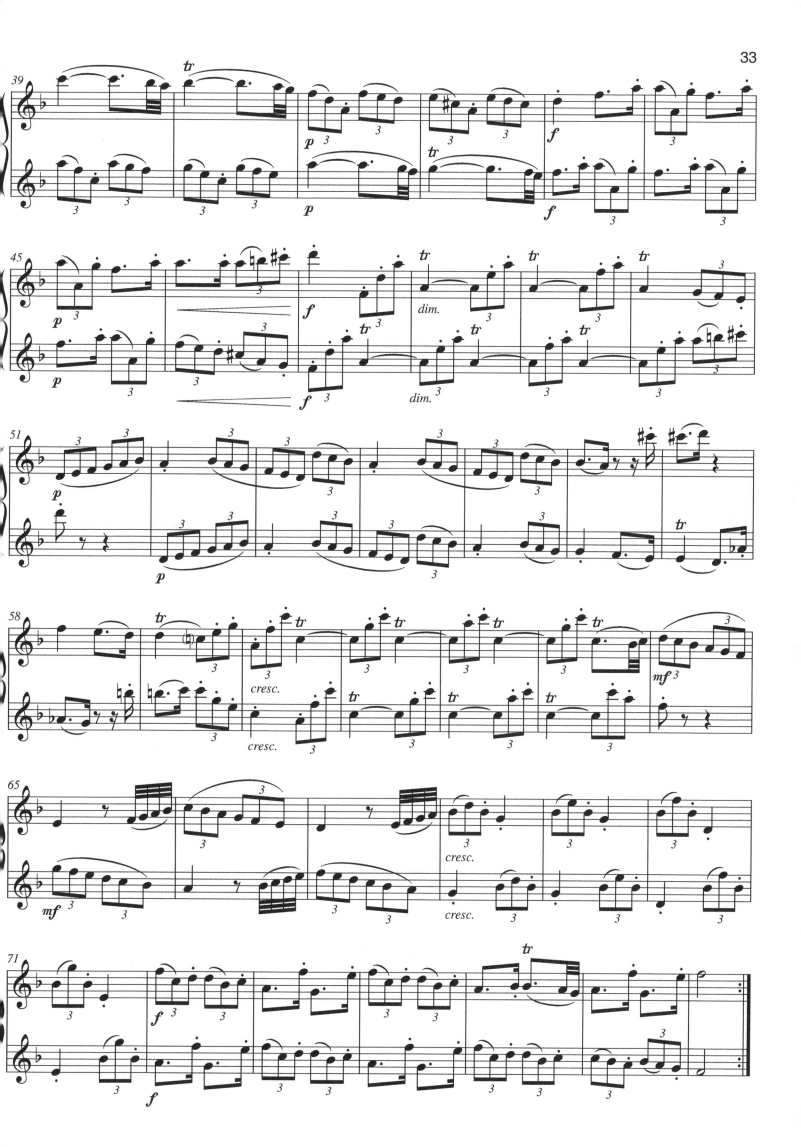

Un poco allegro

14

45

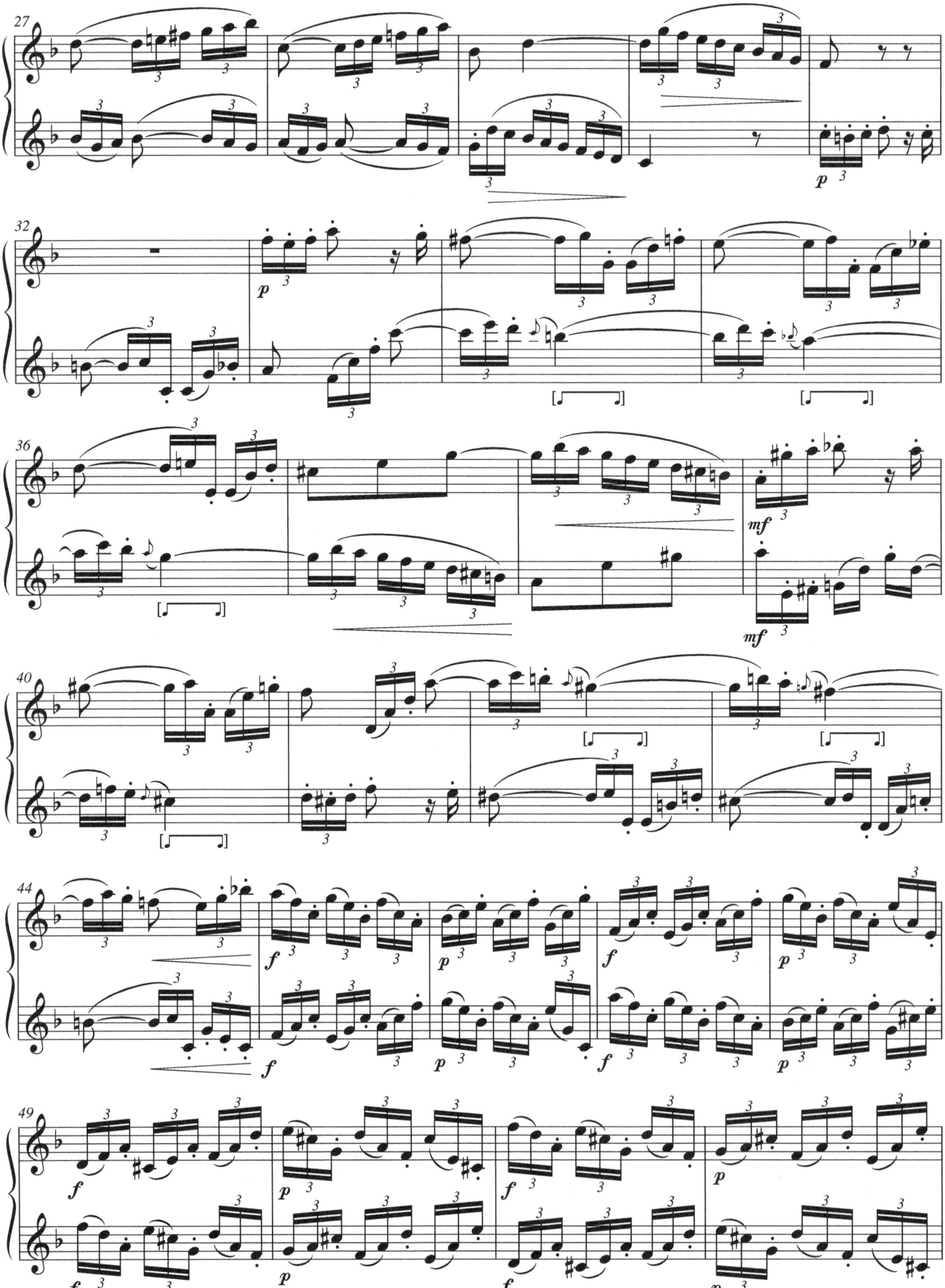

27
p
32
p
36
mf
40
44
f
p
49

Ten Duets

Jean-Marie Leclair
(1697–1764)

Allegro

2

Gigue

Allegro ma non troppo

Minuetto, non troppo allegro

63

Gigue

Allegro ma non poco

10

Thirteen Duets
Canon No. 1

Georg Phillip Telemann
(1681–1767)

The second player begins each section when the first player has reached the sign (𝄋).
The second player finishes each section at the first fermata (𝄐), which should not be observed by the first player.

Canon No. 2

The second player begins each section when the first player has reached the sign (%).
The second player finishes each section at the first fermata (⌢), which should not be observed by the first player.

Soave (Dolce)

94

CLASSIC CLARINET PUBLICATIONS

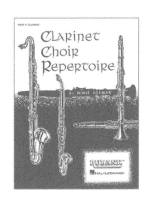

CLASSICAL STUDIES FOR CLARINET
(Voxman)
04470840   Book Only $8.95

INTRODUCING THE ALTO OR BASS CLARINET
(Voxman)
04470850 ....$6.95

KLOZE-LAZARUS METHOD FOR CLARINET
(Whistler)
04470740 ....$8.95

RUBANK METHOD – CLARINET
04470000   Elementary (Hovey) $5.99
04470170   Intermediate (Skornicka/Miller) $5.95
04470310   Advanced Vol. 1 (Voxman/Gower) $6.95
04470320   Advanced Vol. 2 (Voxman/Gower) $6.95

CONCERT AND CONTEST COLLECTION FOR B♭ CLARINET
04471630   Solo Part...$4.99
04471640   Piano Part..$6.99
04002511   Book/CD Pack w/ Accompaniment $14.99

CLARINET CHOIR REPERTOIRE
(Voxman)
04473970   1st B♭...$4.95
04473980   2nd B♭..$4.95
04473990   3rd B♭...$4.95
04474000   4th B♭ (Alternate for Alto Clar.).............$4.95
04474010   Alto Clarinet $4.95
04474020   Bass $4.95
04474030   Full Score $8.95

SUPPLEMENTARY INSTRUMENTAL STUDIES

PARES SCALES
(Parès/rev. Whistler)
Scale studies of the most common major and minor keys designed for individual study and like-instrument class instruction.

04470490   Flute or Piccolo $6.50
04470510   Oboe $6.50
04470520   Bassoon $6.50
04470500   Clarinet..$6.50
04470530   Saxophone..$6.50
04470540   Cornet, Trumpet or Baritone T.C.............$6.50
04470550   French Horn, E♭ Alto or Mellophone $6.50
04470560   Trombone or Baritone B.C.....................$6.50
04470570   E♭ Bass $6.50
04470580   B♭ Bass $6.50
04470590   Marimba, Xylophone or Vibes................$6.50

SELECTED STUDIES
(Voxman)
Advanced etudes, scales, and arpeggios in all major and minor keys for individual study.

04470700   Flute..$6.95
04470710   Oboe $6.95
04470670   Clarinet..$6.95
04470690   Saxophone...$6.95
04470680   Cornet/Trumpet......................................$6.95
04470720   Trombone $6.95
04470730   Baritone B.C. $6.95

SUPPLEMENTARY STUDIES
(R.M. Endresen)
These studies, a series of short etudes designed to improve technique and musicianship, are intended to supplement or follow any elementary method.

04470600   Flute or Piccolo....................................$5.50
04470610   Clarinet...$5.50
04470620   Saxophone...$5.50
04470630   Cornet or Trumpet $5.50
04470640   Trombone $5.50
04470650   French Horn or E♭ Alto $5.50
04470660   E♭ or B♭ Basses..................................$5.50

SELECTED DUETS
(Voxman)
This series of fine duets for like-instruments contains a superb wealth of material designed to demonstrate and reward musical growth and development. (Vol. 1 – Easy to Medium, Vol. 2 – Advanced)

04470920   Flute, Vol. 1..$8.95
04470930   Flute, Vol. 2..$8.99
04470940   Clarinet, Vol. 1 ....$8.99
04470950   Clarinet, Vol. 2 ....$8.95
04470960   Saxophone, Vol. 1 ....$8.95
04470970   Saxophone, Vol. 2 ....$8.95
04470980   Cornet or Trumpet, Vol. 1 ....$8.95
04470990   Cornet or Trumpet, Vol. 2 ....$8.99
04471000   French Horn, Vol. 1...............................$8.95
04471010   French Horn, Vol. 2...............................$8.95
04471020   Trombone or Baritone, Vol. 1 ....$8.95
04471030   Trombone or Baritone, Vol. 2.................$8.95

CHAMBER MUSIC SERIES
(Voxman)
Easy to medium level woodwind trios in score form. Perfect for study, recreation, concert, and contest.

04474540   Three Flutes...$5.95
04474550   Three B♭ Clarinets, Vol. 1 ....$5.99
04474560   Three B♭ Clarinets, Vol. 2 ....$5.99
04474570   Three Saxophones $5.95
04474580   Three Woodwinds, Vol. 1 ....$5.95
04474590   Three Woodwinds, Vol. 2 ....$5.95

01/15